Wonderful Wearable WRAPS

Add new flair and a touch of warmth to all your favorite outfits! These six lacy wraps by Jeannine LaRoche are the perfect fit for your wardrobe. So fun to crochet, each poncho, stole, and shawl is also lovely to wear with everything from blue jeans to dresses. Whether you're on your way to work, enjoying an evening out, or just going for a stroll, remember to wrap yourself in one of these feminine accessories!

Meet Jeannine LaRoche

Jeannine LaRoche once owned a yarn and needlecraft shop. When customers were not able to find a pattern that met their specific needs, Jeannine would design one for them. Her creations caught the attention of a yarn salesman, and after meeting with a vice president of the company, she entered the world of fashion design.

Since those early days, Jeannine's work has appeared in numerous instruction books and national craft magazines. She has also been featured on TV and radio programs in the Boston, Massachusetts area. Although she closed her shop years ago, she continues teaching yarn arts in local schools and church groups.

While working on these shawls, stoles, and poncho, Jeannine went on a cruise, taking some of her designs with her. The passengers seated at her dinner table looked forward to seeing the different wraps she wore each evening.

Jeannine says, "I would like to encourage everyone, young and old, to used their God-given talents to bless others. At 85 years of age, I still teach four classes a week, and students often drop in for extra help. Last year, I moved to Florida and drove my little lime green Volkswagen Beetle (with a moon roof) all the way from California. Life is a challenge—enjoy it!"

LEISURE ARTS, INC.
Maumelle, Arkansas

CROSS STITCH *Shawl*

◼◼▢▢ EASY

Finished Size: 55" (139.5 cm) across top edge
26" (66 cm) deep

MATERIALS

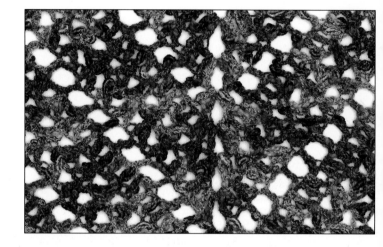

Light Weight Yarn **LIGHT 3**
14 ounces, 400 grams
Crochet hook, size G (4 mm) **or** size needed
for gauge

GAUGE SWATCH: 5" side x 7¼" bottom x 5" side
(12.75 cm x 18.5 cm x
12.75 cm)
Work same as Body for 7 rows.

STITCH GUIDE
CROSS STITCH *(abbreviated Cross St)*
(uses next 2 dc)
Skip next dc, dc in next dc, working **around** dc
just made, dc in skipped dc.

This Shawl begins at the center of the back of the
neck and is worked down. The end of rows form the
top edge.

BODY

Ch 12; join with slip st to form a ring.

Row 1: Ch 3 (**counts as first dc, now and
throughout**), 10 dc in ring; do **not** join: 11 dc.

Row 2 (Right side)**:** Ch 3, turn; 2 dc in first dc, work
Cross St twice, (2 dc, ch 3, 2 dc) in next dc, work
Cross St twice, 3 dc in last dc: 4 Cross Sts, 10 dc
and one ch-3 sp.

Note: Loop a short piece of yarn around any stitch
to mark Row 2 as **right** side.

Row 3: Ch 4 (**counts as first dc plus ch 1, now and
throughout**), turn; dc in first dc, ch 1, (skip next
dc, dc in next dc, ch 1) 4 times, (2 dc, ch 3, 2 dc)
in next ch-3 sp, ch 1, (dc in next dc, ch 1, skip next
dc) 4 times, (dc, ch 1, dc) in last dc: 16 dc and
13 sps.

Instructions continued on page 14.

DIAMONDS & SHELLS *Shawl*

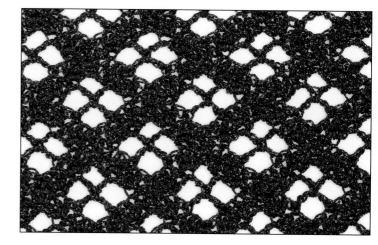

■■□□ EASY

Finished Size: 66" (167.5 cm) across top edge
25½" (65 cm) deep

MATERIALS

Light Weight Yarn
9 ounces, 260 grams
Crochet hook, size G (4 mm) **or** size needed
for gauge

GAUGE SWATCH: 4" side x 6" top x 4" side
(10 cm x 15.25 cm x 10 cm)
Work same as Body for 8 rows.

STITCH GUIDE

TREBLE CROCHET *(abbreviated tr)*
YO twice, insert hook in sp indicated, YO and
pull up a loop (4 loops on hook), (YO and draw
through 2 loops on hook) 3 times.

This Shawl begins at the bottom tip and is worked
up. Shaping is achieved by increasing at the
beginning and the end of each row.

BODY

Row 1 (Right side)**:** Ch 6, 4 dc in fourth ch from
hook: 4 dc.

Note: Loop a short piece of yarn around any stitch
to mark Row 1 as **right** side.

Row 2: Ch 5, turn; 3 dc in first dc, skip next dc, sc
in next dc, skip next dc, 3 dc in last dc: 7 sts and
one ch-5 sp.

Row 3: Ch 5, turn; 3 dc in first dc, sc in next dc,
ch 5, skip next 3 sts, sc in next dc, 3 dc in last
ch-5 sp: 8 sts and 2 ch-5 sps.

Instructions continued on page 15.

FAN & TRELLIS *Stole*

Finished Size: 17½" wide x 60" long
(44.5 cm x 152.5 cm)

MATERIALS

SUPER FINE
1

Super Fine Weight Yarn
7 ounces, 200 grams
Crochet hook, size G (4 mm) **or** size needed
for gauge

Stole is worked holding two strands of yarn together
throughout.

GAUGE: In pattern,
6 ch-5 sps and 12 rows = 5" (12.75 cm)

Gauge Swatch: 5" (12.75 cm) square
Ch 29.
Work same as Stole for 12 rows.
Finish off.

STOLE

Holding two strands of yarn together, ch 89.

Row 1 (Right side)**:** Sc in ninth ch from hook,
★ ch 5, skip next 3 chs, sc in next ch; repeat
from ★ across: 21 sps.

Note: Loop a short piece of yarn around any stitch
to mark Row 1 as **right** side.

Row 2: Ch 5, turn; sc in first ch-5 sp, 7 dc in next
ch-5 sp, ★ sc in next ch-5 sp, ch 5, sc in next
ch-5 sp, 7 dc in next ch-5 sp; repeat from ★ across
to last sp, sc in last sp, (ch 2, dc) in same sp to form
last ch-5 sp: 63 sts and 8 ch-5 sps.

Row 3: Ch 5, turn; ★ † skip next sc and next dc, sc
in next dc, ch 5, skip next 3 dc, sc in next dc, ch 5,
sc in next ch-5 sp †, ch 5; repeat from ★ across to
last 9 sts, then repeat from † to † once: 21 ch-5 sps.

Repeat Rows 2 and 3 for pattern until Stole
measures approximately 60" (152.5 cm) from
beginning ch, ending by working Row 2.

Last Row: Ch 3, turn; ★ † skip next sc and next
dc, sc in next dc, ch 3, skip next 3 dc, sc in next
dc, ch 3, sc in next ch-5 sp †, ch 3; repeat from ★
across to last 9 sts, then repeat from † to † once;
finish off.

Holding 5 strands of yarn together, add fringe in
each sp across short edges of Stole *(Figs. 1a & b,
page 19)*.

LACY *Shawl*

Finished Size: 50" (127 cm) across top edge
33" (84 cm) deep

MATERIALS
Light Weight Yarn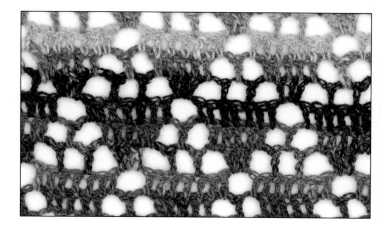
10 ounces, 280 grams,
Crochet hook, size G (4 mm) **or** size needed
for gauge

GAUGE SWATCH: 2³/₄" bottom x 3¹/₂" side x
6" top x 3¹/₂" side (7 cm x
9 cm x 15.25 cm x 9 cm)
Work same as Body for 6 rows.

This Shawl begins at bottom tip and is worked up. Shaping is achieved by increasing at the beginning and the end of each row.

BODY
Ch 14.

Row 1: 3 Dc in fifth ch from hook, ch 2, skip next 2 chs, ★ dc in next ch, ch 2, skip next 2 chs; repeat from ★ once **more**, 3 dc in last ch: 8 dc and 4 sps.

Leave last ch-4 sp at end of each row unworked for fringe placement.

Row 2 (Right side)**:** Ch 4, turn; 2 dc in first dc, dc in next 2 dc and in next ch-2 sp, (ch 2, dc in next ch-2 sp) twice, dc in next 2 dc, 2 dc in last dc: 11 dc and 3 sps.

Note: Loop a short piece of yarn around any stitch to mark Row 2 as **right** side.

Instructions continued on page 16.

PUFF STITCH *Stole*

Finished Size: 16½" wide x 60" long
(42 cm x 152.5 cm)

MATERIALS
Fine Weight Yarn
9 ounces, 260 grams
Crochet hook, size G (4 mm) **or** size needed
for gauge

GAUGE: In pattern, 16 sts = 4" (10 cm);
12 rows = 4½" (11.5 cm)

Gauge Swatch: 4" (10 cm) square
Ch 17.
Work same as Body.

STITCH GUIDE

PUFF STITCH *(abbreviated Puff St)*
(uses one hdc)
YO, insert hook in next hdc, YO and pull up
a loop (3 loops on hook), (YO, insert hook in
same st, YO and pull up loop) twice, YO and
draw through all 7 loops on hook.

BODY
Ch 61.

Row 1: (Right side)**:** Hdc in third ch from hook
(2 skipped chs count as first hdc) and in each ch
across: 60 hdc.

Note: Loop a short piece of yarn around any stitch
to mark Row 1 as **right** side.

Row 2: Ch 2 **(counts as first hdc, now and
throughout)**, turn; work Puff St in next hdc, ★ ch 1,
skip next hdc, work Puff St in next hdc; repeat from
★ across to last 2 hdc, ch 1, skip next hdc, hdc in
last hdc: 29 Puff Sts, 29 ch-1 sps, and 2 hdc.

Row 3: Ch 2, turn; hdc in next ch and in each st
and each ch across: 60 hdc.

Row 4: Ch 2, turn; hdc in next hdc, ★ ch 1, skip
next hdc, hdc in next hdc; repeat from ★ across:
31 hdc and 29 ch-1 sps.

Row 5: Ch 2, turn; hdc in next ch and in each st
and each ch across: 60 hdc.

Rows 6-156: Repeat Rows 2-5, 37 times; then
repeat Rows 2-4 once **more**; do **not** finish off.

Instructions continued on page 17.

SLANT STITCH *Poncho*

◼◼◻◻ EASY

Finished Size: One size fits most women

MATERIALS

MEDIUM 4

Medium Weight Yarn
   13 ounces, 370 grams
Crochet hook, size I (5.5 mm) **or** size needed
   for gauge
Yarn needle

GAUGE: In pattern, 12 sts = 4" (10 cm);
         12 rows = 3³/₄" (9.5 cm)

Gauge Swatch: 4¹/₂" x 3³/₄" (11.5 cm x 9.5 cm)
Ch 15.
Work same as Rectangle for 12 rows.
Finish off.

STITCH GUIDE

TREBLE CROCHET *(abbreviated tr)*
YO twice, insert hook in dc indicated, YO and
pull up a loop (4 loops on hook), (YO and draw
through 2 loops on hook) 3 times.

RECTANGLE (Make 2)
Ch 55.

Row 1: Hdc in third ch from hook **(2 skipped chs count as first hdc)** and in each ch across: 54 hdc.

Row 2 (Right side)**:** Ch 2 **(counts as first hdc, now and throughout)**, turn; hdc in next 2 hdc, dc in next hdc and in each hdc across to last 3 hdc, hdc in last 3 hdc.

Note: Loop a short piece of yarn around any stitch to mark Row 2 as **right** side.

Row 3: Ch 2, turn; hdc in next 2 hdc, ★ skip next dc, dc in next 3 dc, working **around** 3 dc just made, tr in skipped dc; repeat from ★ across to last 3 hdc, hdc in last 3 hdc.

Rows 4 and 5: Ch 2, turn; hdc in next 2 hdc, dc in next st and in each st across to last 3 hdc, hdc in last 3 hdc.

Row 6: Ch 2, turn; hdc in next 2 hdc, ★ skip next dc, dc in next 3 dc, working **around** 3 dc just made, tr in skipped dc; repeat from ★ across to last 3 hdc, hdc in last 3 hdc.

Instructions continued on page 14.

Rows 7 and 8: Ch 2, turn; hdc in next 2 hdc, dc in next st and in each st across to last 3 hdc, hdc in last 3 hdc.

Repeat Rows 3-8 for pattern until Rectangle measures approximately 31" (78.5 cm) from beginning ch, ending by working Row 8.

Last Row: Ch 2, turn; hdc in next st and in each st across; finish off.

FINISHING

With **right** side facing and using diagram as a guide, sew Rectangles together.

Holding 3 strands of yarn together, each 9" (23 cm) long. Add fringe evenly spaced across bottom edges of Poncho *(Figs. 1a & b, page 19)*.

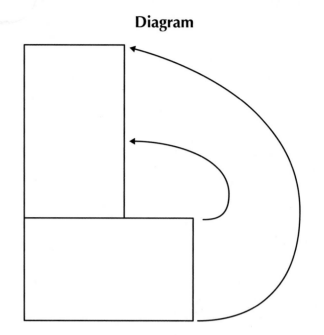

Diagram

CROSS STITCH SHAWL continued from page 2.

Row 4: Ch 3, turn; dc in first dc, dc in next ch-1 sp and in each dc and each ch-1 sp across to next ch-3 sp, (2 dc, ch 3, 2 dc) in ch-3 sp, dc in next dc and in each dc and each ch-1 sp across to last dc, 2 dc in last dc: 34 dc and one ch-3 sp.

Rows 5 and 6: Ch 3, turn; 2 dc in first dc, work Cross Sts across to next ch-3 sp, (2 dc, ch 3, 2 dc) in ch-3 sp, work Cross Sts across to last dc, 3 dc in last dc: 20 Cross Sts, 10 dc and one ch-3 sp.

Row 7: Ch 4, turn; dc in first dc, ch 1, (skip next dc, dc in next dc, ch 1) across to next ch-3 sp, (2 dc, ch 3, 2 dc) in ch-3 sp, ch 1, dc in next dc, ch 1, (skip next dc, dc in next dc, ch 1) across to last 2 dc, skip next dc, (dc, ch 1, dc) in last dc: 32 dc and 29 sps.

Rows 8-51: Repeat Rows 4-7, 11 times: 208 dc and 205 sps.

Finish off.

Holding 6 strands of yarn together, each 12" (30.5 cm) long. Add fringe in every other ch-1 sp across Row 59 of Shawl with one in each of 2 ch-1 sps on each side of the point *(Figs. 1a & b, page 19)*; then work double knotted fringe *(Fig. 1c, page 19)*.

Row 4: Ch 5, turn; 3 dc in first dc, sc in next dc, ch 5, sc in next ch-5 sp, ch 5, skip next sc and next dc, sc in next dc, 3 dc in last ch-5 sp: 9 sts and 3 ch-5 sps.

Row 5: Ch 5, turn; 3 dc in first dc, sc in next dc, skip next dc, 3 dc in next sc, sc in next ch-5 sp, ch 5, sc in next ch-5 sp, 3 dc in next sc, skip next dc, sc in next dc, 3 dc in last ch-5 sp: 16 sts and 2 ch-5 sps.

Row 6: Ch 5, turn; 3 dc in first dc, sc in next dc, ch 5, skip next 3 sts, sc in next dc, skip next dc, 3 dc in next sc, sc in next ch-5 sp, 3 dc in next sc, skip next dc, sc in next dc, ch 5, skip next 3 sts, sc in next dc, 3 dc in last ch-5 sp: 17 sts and 3 ch-5 sps.

Row 7: Ch 5, turn; 3 dc in first dc, sc in next dc, ch 5, sc in next ch-5 sp, ch 5, skip next sc and next dc, sc in next dc, skip next dc, 3 dc in next sc, skip next dc, sc in next dc, ch 5, sc in next ch-5 sp, ch 5, skip next sc and next dc, sc in next dc, 3 dc in last ch-5 sp: 15 sts and 5 ch-5 sps.

Row 8: Ch 5, turn; 3 dc in first dc, sc in next dc, ★ skip next dc, 3 dc in next sc, sc in next ch-5 sp, ch 5, sc in next ch-5 sp, 3 dc in next sc, skip next dc, sc in next dc; repeat from ★ once **more**, 3 dc in last ch-5 sp: 25 sts and 3 ch-5 sps.

Row 9: Ch 5, turn; 3 dc in first dc, sc in next dc, ch 5, skip next 3 sts, sc in next dc, ★ skip next dc, 3 dc in next sc, sc in next ch-5 sp, 3 dc in next sc, skip next dc, sc in next dc, ch 5, skip next 3 sts, sc in next dc; repeat from ★ once **more**, 3 dc in last ch-5 sp: 26 sts and 4 ch-5 sps.

Row 10: Ch 5, turn; 3 dc in first dc, sc in next dc, ch 5, sc in next ch-5 sp, ch 5, skip next sc and next dc, sc in next dc, ★ skip next dc, 3 dc in next sc, skip next dc, sc in next dc, ch 5, sc in next ch-5 sp, ch 5, skip next sc and next dc, sc in next dc; repeat from ★ once **more**, 3 dc in last ch-5 sp: 21 sts and 7 ch-5 sps.

Row 11: Ch 5, turn; 3 dc in first dc, sc in next dc, ★ skip next dc, 3 dc in next sc, sc in next ch-5 sp, ch 5, sc in next ch-5 sp, 3 dc in next sc, skip next dc, sc in next dc; repeat from ★ across to last ch-5 sp, 3 dc in last ch-5 sp: 34 sts and 4 ch-5 sps.

Row 12: Ch 5, turn; 3 dc in first dc, sc in next dc, ch 5, skip next 3 sts, sc in next dc, ★ skip next dc, 3 dc in next sc, sc in next ch-5 sp, 3 dc in next sc, skip next dc, sc in next dc, ch 5, skip next 3 sts, sc in next dc; repeat from ★ across to last ch-5 sp, 3 dc in last ch-5 sp: 35 sts and 5 ch-5 sps.

Row 13: Ch 5, turn; 3 dc in first dc, sc in next dc, ch 5, sc in next ch-5 sp, ch 5, skip next sc and next dc, sc in next dc, ★ skip next dc, 3 dc in next sc, skip next dc, sc in next dc, ch 5, sc in next ch-5 sp, ch 5, skip next sc and next dc, sc in next dc; repeat from ★ across to last ch-5 sp, 3 dc in ch-5 sp: 27 sts and 9 ch-5 sps.

Rows 14-82: Repeat Rows 11-13, 23 times.

Edging: Ch 3 (**counts as first dc**), turn; 2 dc in first dc, sc in next dc, skip next dc, 2 dc in next sc, sc in next ch-5 sp, ch 2, sc in next ch-5 sp, 2 dc in next sc, ★ skip next dc, sc in next dc, skip next dc, 2 dc in next sc, sc in next ch-5 sp, ch 2, sc in next ch-5 sp, 2 dc in next sc; repeat from ★ across to last 3 dc, skip next dc, sc in last 2 dc; working in ch-5 sp at end of rows, sc in first ch-5 sp, (7 tr in next ch-5 sp, sc in next ch-5 sp) across to bottom tip, 9 tr in next ch-5 sp on Row 1, (sc in next ch-5 sp, 7 tr in next ch-5 sp) across; join with slip st to first dc, finish off.

LACY SHAWL continued from page 8.

Row 3: Ch 4, turn; 3 dc in first dc, dc in next 4 dc and in next ch-2 sp, ch 2, dc in next ch-2 sp and in next 4 dc, 3 dc in last dc: 16 dc and 2 sps.

Row 4: Ch 4, turn; 3 dc in first dc, ch 2, skip next 2 dc, dc in next dc, ch 2, skip next dc, dc in next dc, ch 2, 3 dc in next ch-2 sp, ch 2, skip next 2 dc, dc in next dc, ch 2, skip next dc, dc in next dc, ch 2, skip next 2 dc, 3 dc in last dc: 13 dc and 7 sps.

Row 5: Ch 4, turn; 2 dc in first dc, dc in next 2 dc and in next ch-2 sp, (ch 2, dc in next ch-2 sp) twice, dc in next 3 dc and in next ch-2 sp, (ch 2, dc in next ch-2 sp) twice, dc in next 2 dc, 2 dc in last dc: 17 dc and 5 sps.

Row 6: Ch 4, turn; 3 dc in first dc, dc in next 4 dc and in next ch-2 sp, ch 2, dc in next ch-2 sp, dc in next 5 dc and in next ch-2 sp, ch 2, dc in next ch-2 sp and in next 4 dc, 3 dc in last dc: 23 dc and 3 sps.

Row 7: Ch 4, turn; 3 dc in first dc, ch 2, skip next 2 dc, dc in next dc, ch 2, skip next dc, dc in next dc, ch 2, ★ 3 dc in next ch-2 sp, ch 2, skip next 2 dc, dc in next dc, ch 2, skip next dc, dc in next dc, ch 2; repeat from ★ once **more**, skip next 2 dc, 3 dc in last dc: 18 dc and 10 sps.

Row 8: Ch 4, turn; 2 dc in first dc, dc in next 2 dc and in next ch-2 sp, (ch 2, dc in next ch-2 sp) twice, ★ dc in next 3 dc and in next ch-2 sp, (ch 2, dc in next ch-2 sp) twice; repeat from ★ once **more**, dc in next 2 dc, 2 dc in last dc: 23 dc and 7 sps.

Row 9: Ch 4, turn; 3 dc in first dc, dc in next 4 dc and in next ch-2 sp, ch 2, ★ dc in next ch-2 sp, dc in next 5 dc and in next ch-2 sp, ch 2; repeat from ★ once **more**, dc in next ch-2 sp and in next 4 dc, 3 dc in last dc: 30 dc and 4 sps.

Row 10: Ch 4, turn; 3 dc in first dc, ch 2, skip next 2 dc, dc in next dc, ch 2, skip next dc, dc in next dc, ch 2, ★ 3 dc in next ch-2 sp, ch 2, skip next 2 dc, dc in next dc, ch 2, skip next dc, dc in next dc, ch 2; repeat from ★ across to last 3 dc, skip next 2 dc, 3 dc in last dc: 23 dc and 13 sps.

Row 11: Ch 4, turn; 2 dc in first dc, dc in next 2 dc and in next ch-2 sp, (ch 2, dc in next ch-2 sp) twice, ★ dc in next 3 dc and in next ch-2 sp, (ch 2, dc in next ch-2 sp) twice; repeat from ★ across to last 3 dc, dc in next 2 dc, 2 dc in last dc: 29 dc and 9 sps.

Row 12: Ch 4, turn; 3 dc in first dc, dc in next 4 dc and in next ch-2 sp, ch 2, dc in next ch-2 sp, ★ dc in next 5 dc and in next ch-2 sp, ch 2, dc in next ch-2 sp; repeat from ★ across to last 5 dc, dc in next 4 dc, 3 dc in last dc: 37 dc and 5 sps.

Rows 13-72: Repeat Rows 10-12, 20 times.

Finish off.

Holding 5 strands of yarn together, each 9" (23 cm) long. Add fringe in each unworked ch-4 sp across short edges of Shawl *(Figs. 1a & b, page 19)*.

EDGING

Row 1: Ch 2, turn; working across top edge, hdc in next ch and in each st and each ch across to last hdc, 3 hdc in last hdc; working across long edge, work 237 hdc evenly spaced across end of rows: 299 hdc.

Row 2: Ch 2, turn; work Puff St in next hdc, (ch 2, skip next 2 hdc, work Puff St in next hdc) across to last hdc of next 3-hdc group, hdc in last hdc, leave remaining 59 hdc across top edge unworked: 80 Puff Sts, 79 ch-2 sps, and 2 hdc.

Row 3: Ch 2, turn; working across same long edge only, hdc in next Puff St and in each ch and each Puff St across; working across bottom edge, 2 sc in end of Row 2, sc in end of Row 1; working around beginning ch and in sp **between** hdc *(Fig. A)*, sc in each sp across; ch 3, working across long edge, work 239 hdc evenly spaced across end of rows: 542 sts.

Fig. A

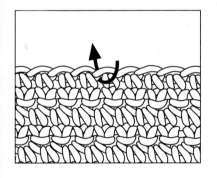

Row 4: Ch 2, turn; working across same long edge only, work Puff St in next hdc, ★ ch 2, skip next 2 hdc, work Puff St in next hdc; repeat from ★ across to last st, hdc in last st, leave remaining sts unworked: 80 Puff Sts, 79 ch-2 sps, and 2 hdc.

Row 5: Ch 2, turn; hdc in next Puff St and in each ch and each Puff St across to last hdc, 2 hdc in last hdc; 2 sc in end of Row 4, sc in end of Row 3; working in sp **between** hdc *(Fig. B)*, sc in each sp across; sc in same hdc as 3-hdc group, 2 sc in end of Row 2, slip st in next hdc; finish off.

Fig. B

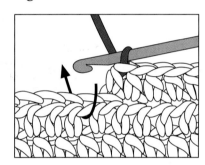

GENERAL *Instructions*

ABBREVIATIONS

ch(s)	chain(s)
cm	centimeters
dc	double crochet(s)
hdc	half double crochet(s)
mm	millimeters
sc	single crochet(s)
sp(s)	space(s)
st(s)	stitch(es)
tr	treble crochet(s)
YO	yarn over

★ — work instructions following ★ as many **more** times as indicated in addition to the first time.

† to † — work all instructions from first † to second † **as many** times as specified.

( ) or [ ] — work enclosed instructions **as many** times as specified by the number immediately following **or** work all enclosed instructions in the stitch or space indicated **or** contains explanatory remarks.

colon (:) — the number(s) given after a colon at the end of a row denote(s) the number of stitches or spaces you should have on that row.

■□□□ BEGINNER	Projects for first-time crocheters using basic stitches. Minimal shaping.
■■□□ EASY	Projects using yarn with basic stitches, repetitive stitch patterns, simple color changes, and simple shaping and finishing.
■■■□ INTERMEDIATE	Projects using a variety of techniques, such as basic lace patterns or color patterns, mid-level shaping and finishing.
■■■■ EXPERIENCED	Projects with intricate stitch patterns, techniques and dimension, such as non-repeating patterns, multi-color techniques, fine threads, small hooks, detailed shaping and refined finishing.

Yarn Weight Symbol & Names	LACE 0	SUPER FINE 1	FINE 2	LIGHT 3	MEDIUM 4	BULKY 5	SUPER BULKY 6
Type of Yarns in Category	Fingering, 10-count crochet thread	Sock, Fingering Baby	Sport, Baby	DK, Light Worsted	Worsted, Afghan, Aran	Chunky, Craft, Rug	Bulky, Roving
Crochet Gauge* Ranges in Single Crochet to 4" (10 cm)	32-42 double crochets**	21-32 sts	16-20 sts	12-17 sts	11-14 sts	8-11 sts	5-9 sts
Advised Hook Size Range	Steel*** 6,7,8 Regular hook B-1	B-1 to E-4	E-4 to 7	7 to I-9	I-9 to K-10.5	K-10.5 to M-13	M-13 and larger

*GUIDELINES ONLY: The chart above reflects the most commonly used gauges and hook sizes for specific yarn categories.

** Lace weight yarns are usually crocheted on larger-size hooks to create lacy openwork patterns. Accordingly, a gauge range is difficult to determine. Always follow the gauge stated in your pattern.

*** Steel crochet hooks are sized differently from regular hooks–the higher the number the smaller the hook, which is the reverse of regular hook sizing.

CROCHET TERMINOLOGY	
UNITED STATES	**INTERNATIONAL**
slip stitch (slip st)	= single crochet (sc)
single crochet (sc)	= double crochet (dc)
half double crochet (hdc)	= half treble crochet (htr)
double crochet (dc)	= treble crochet(tr)
treble crochet (tr)	= double treble crochet (dtr)
double treble crochet (dtr)	= triple treble crochet (ttr)
triple treble crochet (tr tr)	= quadruple treble crochet (qtr)
skip	= miss

GAUGE

Exact gauge is **essential** for proper size. Before beginning your project, make the sample swatch given in the individual instructions in the yarn and hook specified. After completing the swatch, measure it, counting your stitches and rows carefully. If your swatch is larger or smaller than specified, make another, changing hook size to get the correct gauge. Keep trying until you find the size hook that will give you the specified gauge.

FRINGE

Cut a piece of cardboard 3" (7.5 cm) wide and ½" (12 mm) longer than you want your finished fringe to be. Wind the yarn loosely and evenly lengthwise around the cardboard until the card is filled, then cut across one end; repeat as needed.

Hold together as many strands of yarn as specified for the finished fringe; fold in half. With **wrong** side facing and using a crochet hook, draw the folded end up through a stitch or space and pull the loose ends through the folded end *(Fig. 1a)*; draw the knot up **tightly** *(Fig. 1b)*. Repeat spacing as instructed in individual instructions.

After completing fringe specified in individual instructions, lay piece flat on a hard surface and trim the ends.

Fig. 1a

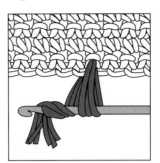

Fig. 1b

For double knotted fringe:
Divide each group in half and knot together with half of next group *(Fig. 1c)*.

Fig. 1c

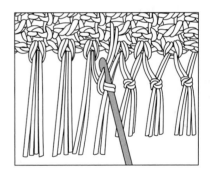

CROCHET HOOKS													
U.S.	B-1	C-2	D-3	E-4	F-5	G-6	H-8	I-9	J-10	K-10½	N	P	Q
Metric - mm	2.25	2.75	3.25	3.5	3.75	4	5	5.5	6	6.5	9	10	15

We have made every effort to ensure that these instructions are accurate and complete. We cannot, however, be responsible for human error, typographical mistakes, or variations in individual work.

Production Team: Instructional/Technical Editor - Lois J. Long; Editorial Writer - Susan McManus Johnson; Senior Graphic Artist - Lora Puls; Graphic Artist - Kara Darling and Becca Snider; Photo Stylist - Cora Holdaway; and Photographer - Jason Masters.